St. Philomena

SAINT PHILOMENA

The Story of a Stubborn Little Princess

by
Courtney C. Filomena Lee

With Illustrations by
Diana Holcombe

SERIF PRESS
2013

SERIF PRESS
Pittsburgh
serifpress.com

This one is for you, Mom. Words are not enough to thank you for helping me do this, especially through all the times that I just wanted to give up. Thanks for always being there for me and helping me fulfill my dreams.

CONTENTS

PART 2: WORLDWIDE DEVOTIONS
TO SAINT PHILOMENA

PROLOGUE
The Finding in the Catacombs

May 24, 1802 was not only the Feast of Our Lady Help of Christians, but also the day excavators in the Priscilla Catacombs would remember as the day they unearthed an ancient tomb. While digging near the "Greek Chapel" they stumbled upon an amazing discovery. It was an unopened grave sealed with three terra cotta tiles. They stopped digging immediately, and Fr. Filippo Ludovici, the official overseer of all excavations, was notified.

The tomb was officially recorded by Fr. Ludovici the next day. Painted on the three tiles were the words, *"Lumena Pax Te Cum Fi."* In order to understand the phrase, the tiles had to be rearranged. The first tile should have been the last so it said, "Peace to you Philomena!" Some scholars believe that another translation would read simply, "Peace to you darling!" Roughly drawn between the words were some significant symbols: a lily, two arrows, and an anchor.

The tiles were removed and the grave opened to reveal some small bones, a fractured skull, and a broken vial still containing dried blood. The vial was embedded in the concrete that sealed the tomb, something done by early Christians to signify martyrdom. Doctors and surgeons determined that the relics were those of a young girl no more than twelve or thirteen years old. Thus began the wonderful story of an ideal role model for the youth of the world.

PART ONE
St. Philomena's Story

CHAPTER ONE
A Small Part
of Greece

Long ago, there lived a prince and a princess. They are my parents and I am their daughter, Philomena. I live now with my Heavenly Spouse in Paradise, and I would like to tell you my story.

My parents were rulers of a small island called Corfu in Greece near the end of the third century. My mother had been barren for many years. My parents worshiped idols day and night in vain in hopes of having a child. All of this changed when Publius, a doctor from Rome, came to work in the palace for my father. Publius was a devout Christian and was pained to see my parents offering everything they had to the false gods of Greece.

One day, not too long after his arrival, Publius was alone with my parents. "Your Highnesses," he said, "I have noticed your ways of worship and would like to teach you about the God I worship. He is all-kind and all-merciful and cares so much for His people. If you convert, perhaps God will bless you with the child that you long for."

My parents were overcome with excitement

about the Faith and worked eagerly to learn more. As Publius taught my parents about Christianity, they rid the palace of the idols and images of the false gods. They were soon ready to be baptized. Publius promised he would pray for them so they would continue to grow ever holier.

The day of their baptism, my parents were preparing and talking anxiously together.

"I am so nervous," my mother said, combing her long dark hair, her slender hands shaking.

"Publius said God might send us a child if we converted. Even if Publius is wrong, isn't it wonderful that God knows and cares for us?" my father pointed out.

"Yes, it is a good feeling," my mother said putting a jeweled comb into her hair. "It brings joy to my heart to know that Publius is teaching everyone in the palace about Christianity. It makes me feel stronger just knowing others will be on the right path as well."

My father smiled as he fastened his sandals, "Yes, that is a comforting thought, isn't it?"

Just then, a messenger entered the room, "Publius is here, Your Highness."

"Send him in," my father said, rising from his seat.

Publius entered the room beaming happily.

"How are you doing?" he asked gently. My parents had asked him to be informal with them so he did not bow.

"We are a little uneasy, Publius," my mother answered truthfully with a small smile.

"You have no need to worry," said Publius. "I know that both of you are ready to be baptized and become strong Christian examples for your people. God will grant you the graces you need. All you have to do is ask Him."

The ceremony was magnificent and very reverent. Everyone wore white as a symbol of new life. My father was baptized first. When the water was poured onto his head, he felt a new strength begin to grow in him. My mother also felt this strange power. Publius had told my parents that the Holy Spirit would be working to make them good Christians from the start.

The celebration that followed was marvelous and countless people traveled from all over the island to attend. My father and mother were overcome with joy in becoming Christians, and all of their subjects were pleased to see their prince and princess happy at last.

Not too long after their baptisms, my mother found herself with child. My parents' hearts were filled with deep gratitude and delight.

They wasted no time in finding Publius. They found him in the church teaching about Christ. They ran to him and my mother knelt with her hands in his lap, weeping. Publius was worried at first, but when she looked up to meet his eyes, he saw happiness and humility.

"Thank you for teaching us about God and about Christianity, Publius, for without you we would not know true happiness," my mother said as a beautiful smile lit her features.

My father offered him a high position in court, but once again Publius turned him down humbly saying, "My only reward will be God's favor, my prince."

At this, my father nodded. He had already suspected that answer but was now wondering what else to offer this wonderful man of God.

"Do not strain your mind thinking of what to give me," Publius said gently. "Rather give thanks to God."

Without hesitation, my parents went to a private part of the church and offered prayers of thanksgiving, while Publius continued to teach the people about Christianity and the path to Heaven.

CHAPTER TWO
A Great Light,
A Small Princess

When I was born, my parents named me Lumena, a reference to the light of faith that I had been to them in their painful years of being childless.

I was born in 291 A.D and the whole island celebrated that day. I was put into a gilded cradle and rocked to sleep by my father.

On the day of my baptism, my parents gave me the name Philomena, which means "Daughter of Light." That night the most splendid feast ever held took place in the palace garden. Everyone wore their finest and the courtyard was soon filled with joyful people. My mother often told me that Publius was indeed present but remained quiet and undiscovered until my father asked him to come up on the dais. Of course, most everyone already knew Publius, but my father believed it to be an important part of the ceremony. My mother was so beautiful; many could hardly believe she had just had a child not so very long ago.

Since I was such a blessing to my parents, they rarely let me out of their sight. I thoroughly enjoyed all of the love that I received from them. However, I was still allowed a normal life even with my parents' constant protection and devotion.

One day, my mother was watching me play in one of the gardens, as I often did, when she realized it was about to rain.

"Philomena, I think that we should go back inside now," my mother said gently.

Now, you must understand that I loved my mother, trying always to be obedient to her, but I was also very strong-willed, one of God's most challenging gifts to manage. From the time I could crawl, I was like this, and at this time, when I was only about three, it was the same.

"No," I stated, shaking my head furiously, "I do not want to go in; I want to stay and play with my new doll."

My doll was especially pretty, and unlike most Grecian dolls, she was painted with bright paints to make her seem as though she wore a chiton, sandals and jewelry.

My mother was wise, knowing my weak spot, and said, "Philomena, you do not want to make God unhappy by disobeying me, do you?"

Again, I shook my head and tears came to my eyes. "No, I am sorry, mother." With this, I threw my arms around my mother's neck, and she carried me in.

"When you do the right thing, you make God so happy, dear Philomena," my mother said as we took the path back to the palace.

"All that I want is to make God happy, Mother," I said, my tears drying up.

At this, my mother smiled sweetly and said, "Philomena, we should always try to make God happy, even in the littlest things. Sometimes it is hard, but God will help us when we need Him."

We often had these kinds of talks when I

was younger, and even when I was older my mother would tell me about God and His wonderful plan for all of us.

My father often took me with him to important meetings in the throne room. My mother told me that I lightened the serious mood of all royal meetings by sitting beside my father on his large throne. Sometimes my father had me sit with my mother on her throne so that certain visitors would not think he was distracted or uncaring. Most people, however, knew of my parents' great love for me and always smiled at me and asked me the type of questions that people ask small children.

I was not a child who was easily distracted, but I often daydreamed about Heaven and how beautiful and fun everything would be there. I loved most anything that made me laugh. I also enjoyed playing small tricks on people. Once I knocked on my parents' door and ran. I repeated the trick several times until my mother stood in the doorway and caught me. She had a smile on her face, and I knew at once that she was happy. My mother told me that I had taken her away from a boring task and made her laugh; as a result, I was not in trouble.

One of my best friends was the outdoors. I loved running and playing with the servants' children and spending time in the gardens. I also loved animals, especially horses. My father often let me ride with him on his horse, since it was not proper for me to ride because I was a girl.

I was a child with vast amounts of energy, and I spent a great deal of time weaving, something all Greek girls were taught at a young age. I made belts and other items for my mother and other women in the palace. In turn, my mother loved dressing me up in silk chitons of bright colors imported from other countries and jewelry made from the finest gems. I loved these things since they were gifts from my mother, but they were not as important to me as they were to her.

I loved God and tried to please Him by keeping the Commandments and by loving everyone around me as best I could.

CHAPTER
THREE
A Sacred Promise

Publius left to return to Rome when I was still quite young. My mother wept many tears and my father was unusually quiet. Publius embraced my mother then turned to my father and embraced him as well. My father had given me a pouch of gold coins to give to Publius and I approached him with the pouch held before me.

"No, no, dear little princess," Publius said, crouching so that we met eye to eye, "you keep the coins to buy nice things for God's church."

"Publius......." my father began in protest.

Publius held up his hand, the normal serene look on his face, "Your Highness, I cannot accept money for doing the Lord's work."

"I have a gift for you that I made," I quietly told the doctor. I gave him a woven cross about the length of his hand. Publius took the small gift in his palm and tucked it inside his Roman toga.

"So it will always be as near to my heart as you are Philomena," Publius said, his eyes glassy from the effort to hold back his tears. I forgot everything my mother had taught me about being a princess and flung my arms around the good doctor's neck. Publius returned my embrace. I then stepped back and ran to my mother in tears. We watched Publius leave the palace through the main gate and then returned inside, sadness filling our hearts and the hearts of everyone in the palace.

Over the years, I was raised to be a holy child, and upon Publius's departure, I spent a lot of my time in the church, praying to God to bless the people around me. I loved bringing flowers to the altar and setting them before the large marble statue of Jesus.

One bright sunny day I brought a lovely bunch of flowers into the church. As I knelt to place them at the foot of the altar, I suddenly realized that, unlike my mother, I could not marry. I loved Jesus so much and all I wanted was to be His spouse forever.

As I knelt in the empty church I whispered,

"Dear Jesus, I love You so much and I want only You to be my husband. Please help me to be a good girl every day and obey my parents and all the good and holy people around me. Lord Jesus, please keep me safe and help me to be strong during temptation and trials. Please keep me steadfast during sufferings and help me all the days that I live. Amen."

Little did I know that great trials were to come later in my life and how much I was going to suffer for my Heavenly Spouse.

I was ten years old the day I vowed my virginity to God.

I knelt there for a long time until my mother came in search of me. When I heard her calling me I knew I had stayed too long and worried her. I hastily arose and went to my mother, who was at the temple door. I rushed into her open arms and she held me tight.

"I was afraid I'd lost you, dearest daughter!"

my mother exclaimed.

I smiled weakly. "No, mother, I lost count of time and overstayed my visit to Jesus. I'm sorry to have frightened you."

I smiled up at her and she returned my grin then took my hand.

"Your father wants us to meet him for the midday meal on the beach," my mother told me. I followed happily, for I loved the beach and enjoyed standing at the edge of the water while I collected seashells.

The years wore on, and I was soon a well-mannered girl of twelve, and much discussion revolved around my marriage. By my thirteenth birthday celebration, my parents still had not decided whom I should marry, and it was causing quite a commotion in my innocent way of life.

Since I was of marrying age, I wasn't allowed to go anywhere without my mother, my father or a trusted servant. Therefore, my life changed drastically, and I truly wasn't fond of it. I tried everything to persuade my parents to allow me to roam on my own, but they stood firm. Eventually I gave up and trudged around with someone always in my shadow.

I never told anyone of my promise to Jesus. When my parents or anyone else talked of whom I would marry, I would simply smile and say nothing. I was determined to keep my promise but was not sure how to tell my parents.

CHAPTER
FOUR
A Trip to Rome

In the spring, when I was thirteen, alarming news reached us in Corfu: an unjust war was about to be waged on our country by the Roman Empire. Of course, my father knew that our country could never win against the Romans in a war and he was deeply concerned about the safety of our people.

My father sat through countless meetings with the lords of the palace and his weariness showed when he kissed me goodnight at the end of every day. My mother would advise him on everything he told her about the meetings that had taken place that day. He would listen with renewed interest to her suggestions. I was always listening so I would know what was happening, since they rarely told me much about things such as war and treaties.

In the days that followed, my parents decided to travel to Rome to seek an audience with Emperor Diocletian. Although Diocletian was known to be a harsh and unforgiving man, they knew that going to him was their only real hope. They decided to risk their lives so that our country might be spared.

"We must go," my father said to my mother as he paced while she sat weaving at a table. I was gathering flowers just far enough away that I could barely make out their voices.

"What will we do about Philomena? I don't know if she should travel that far from our safe haven here in Corfu," my mother said anxiously.

"She must come!" my father said pounding his fist on the table making my mother's balls of wool bounce.

I was startled and looked up from picking flowers. My mother smiled somewhat absently at me, I smiled back then turned away. I was worried and shaken by my father's anger at the whole situation. He had been a little irritable for a few weeks now, and my mother had been given multiple opportunities to exercise her unfailing patience.

Then his tone lowered and I could barely hear them anymore.

"Besides, it won't be safe for long if the Romans invade Corfu. I feel strongly that we should not leave Philomena here without us. I can't even think about being away from our daughter for that long," my father said in a gentle tone as he gazed at me.

"I agree," my mother said as she turned her head to look at me.

I could feel my father watching me, and I turned from my flower picking, smiled and waved at him. He waved back, but his smile did not reach his eyes.

"Shall I call for your secretary so that you can dictate a message to the Emperor?" my mother offered.

"Yes. I would like you and Philomena to start preparations to leave," my father said softly, his anger seemingly gone for the time.

My mother nodded then rose and called out to me. I hurried to her side, and we went indoors to begin preparations, as my father had requested.

Preparing for a journey was not an easy task for royal people and often took a few weeks, sometimes even months. Those who would accompany us numbered about one hundred people, which was the most my father could afford to take from our almost defenseless state.

I packed my things in large woven baskets with the help of some servants and my mother. I was supposed to look nice the whole time we would be in Rome. That meant no old chitons to run about in and, in essence, no running about at all. I wasn't too disappointed; my parents told me that there would be a whole city to explore. I packed twenty silken chitons, three mantles, four pairs of sandals, and my finest jewelry. My personal items included lotions, perfumes, powders and oils that my mother insisted on me bringing.

My mother and I would travel in a litter carried by eight of our strongest servants until we reached the docks. From there, we would travel by ship to Rome. The litter would then carry us to the Emperor's palace.

My father would ride on his horse most of the way, leading the army that numbered about fifty men, all mounted. Next in the procession would be our litter, behind us would be my father's advisors, and last would be our servants and all of our belongings.

I knew it would be a long journey that would last for some time. Still, I was looking forward to it, since I would see more of the world than most other Greek girls.

I had been praying for my parents in the church every day, especially my father, who was so concerned about the Romans invading. Due to the huge distractions, they seemed to have forgotten my marriage discussions, which pleased me greatly.

CHAPTER FIVE
A Long Journey

Three days later, the journey began very early in the morning after a special celebration in the church. I enjoyed the celebration, especially when we were all blessed by the priest with a blessing just for travelers.

Then the long journey began. My mother

climbed into the litter and extended her hand to help me in. A patch of red poppies caught my eye and I jolted off, grabbing a handful and sprinting to the church in a most unlady-like fashion. I placed them gently at the foot of my favorite statue, bent to kiss the cool marble floor and dashed back to the courtyard where the chaos was still being sorted. I was suddenly ashamed; my mother would be upset with the way I had run to the church.

To my surprise, my mother was smiling when I returned and I grinned back at her.

"That's my daughter, the royal princess of Corfu," she said to me teasingly.

I simply laughed and took her hand, nearly tripping on my way into the litter.

The litter was wood with gold inlaid in the small pillars that supported the roof. The sides were draped in purple silk fabric to symbolize our royal status. The litter was carved with scenes from the Scriptures, such as the Ten Commandments being given to Moses on Mount Sinai. The inside of the litter was padded with soft silk covered cushions, and there were plenty of pillows for us to stretch out on. It was large enough for both of us to recline and still have a little bit of room left for a tray of food.

My father led the way on his handsome white horse that bore him nobly. My father wore clothes that were stamped with the Corfu crest. His horse's saddle blanket matched the color of my father's garments. Fifty soldiers followed my father, and I was so proud of him. I loved the festivity and fun, even if it was for a very serious reason.

The people of Corfu lined the streets of the city to see us off and my mother and I waved and smiled at them. They were all dressed in the common white or brown chitons that were either wool or cotton. The people knew the grave reason for our journey but still threw flowers and cheered happily for us as we passed through on our way to the docks.

The journey took several days, and I loved it! We traveled aboard three ships: one for the main body of soldiers, one for our family and our servants and one for the horses, carts, our litter and a few other servants.

I was never idle and rarely still. I loved to play with the few other children on our ship, and my parents never worried about me, since I was always near enough that one of them could see or hear me.

Though the journey did not last long, many of the adults were grumpy and tired and their children had more work to do. I lost my play-mates to their duties, but I did not pout or complain. Instead, I prayed, wove, and assisted my mother in overseeing the peoples' needs.

After each day, my father would come to our cabin, and I would rush to greet him. He would hug me and kiss my forehead. I would take his cloak then hurry off to put it away while my mother greeted my father.

At the beginning and end of everyday, everyone on the ship prayed together. I prayed that Jesus and all His angels and saints would help us in Rome. After all, in Rome many had gone to their death just for being Christian or refusing the Emperor. I prayed for the souls of the people that had died for their faith. I also prayed for my virginity to remain always perfect in God's sight and for my parents to be successful in their efforts to save our homeland.

CHAPTER SIX
Rome at Last

The final leg of our journey was here and we eagerly pressed on toward Rome, anxious to see the capital of the world. Everyone was filled with renewed energy and hurried about their work with anticipation.

The last night of our voyage was spent at the mouth of the Tiber River. We docked at Ostia, the main seaport of Rome, and spent the night aboard the ship.

My mother and I took special care with our hair that evening and laid out our most elegant chitons to wear into Rome. My mother and father fell asleep quickly but I was wide-awake. I burrowed beneath my woven blankets and prayed for my father to always be led by God and for my mother to stand by him courageously. Last of all, I prayed for nobleness to fulfill my vow to Jesus forever.

Horns blared from the ranks of our escort as we entered Rome on an early April day. Our guards marched smartly behind my father, who looked magnificent on his horse. My mother held a perfumed cloth to her nose to block out the wretched smells of Rome and kept muttering about how blessed we were to be above the filth of the streets.

My mother had me dressed up quite nicely, and I suspected she would make me do so the entire time we were in Rome. I did not mind too much, because I wanted to make her happy.

I was eagerly taking in every detail of Rome that I saw. It was not as tropically beautiful as my home island, but the structures were remarkable and the wealthy homes were stunning and clean looking. The marketplace we passed through was busy and crowded with men, women and children, not to mention dozens of animals.

I memorized everything I saw and pointed things out to my mother that I thought were amazing. She was strangely quiet and scarcely nodded to my excited pointing. No doubt, the meeting with the Emperor was weighing on her mind heavily. I realized she was upset despite her efforts to hide it. I tried to distract her but she simply put her arm around my shoulders and we sat in silence.

At the palace, our litter was placed on the ground and we got out. I was eager to stretch my legs, but my mother grabbed my hand, and we went in search of my father. We followed him and a few of our guards to the large palace door, where we were met by a Roman guard on duty.

My father, through his translator, explained who we were, and the guard opened the door and led us to the throne room. The guard we were following took us through another set of doors. These ones led to the largest room I had ever been inside during my short lifetime. At the end of the room sat a stern-looking man on a golden throne. He wore a jeweled crown and a strange Roman toga that was different from our elegant chitons.

All of a sudden, a loud voice proclaimed our arrival. "The Prince of Corfu here to see the royal Emperor Diocletian!"

My father walked with his noble head held high and his eyes fixed cleverly on the Emperor of the greatest Empire on earth. My mother and I followed in a similar way as our guards continued behind us. We all bowed at the waist when we reached the foot of the Emperor's throne.

"Prince of Corfu," the Emperor spoke in a deep voice, "give me a good reason why I should not tighten my stranglehold on your small nation!"

My father went on to plead our case while the Emperor stared at me with a fixed gaze. I kept my eyes on my father, who was speaking bravely to the Emperor.

"Good Prince, worry no more!" Emperor Diocletian proclaimed loudly, cutting off my father while he still spoke. "You will have the Imperial Forces for your protection. I ask only for the hand of your daughter in marriage."

I was shocked into silence and could not find my tongue to tell my parents I had vowed my purity to Jesus.

My father was astounded with his good fortune and accepted the Emperor's offer immediately. I stood there numb and barely able to think as I heard my parents repeatedly shower thanks on the Emperor. The Emperor sat back on his throne, looking down at me with a greedy stare that made me shudder.

Oh dearest Jesus, help me, I prayed silently.

We were quickly escorted out of the palace as my parents joyfully clung to one another. They had saved our country and, at the same time, gained the highest status for me, their only child.

We hastened home that very day and the trip was much faster. I tried to tell them about my vow to Jesus but they were not listening. They kept saying we would speak about it at home and not to worry.

When we reached home, I told my parents of my consecration to the Lord. My father told me that I had been too young to make such a decision without his consent and thus the war began between my parents and me.

"Philomena, you must marry him, otherwise Corfu is doomed!" my mother pleaded with me one day not long after our return.

I shook my head firmly and said, "Mother, I consecrated myself to God, and to Him I will remain ever faithful."

CHAPTER SEVEN
Philomena's Decision

My parents begged and pleaded with me every day until they wearied seeing my resolution.

I knew that my parents wanted me to marry Diocletian because they believed it would be best for our people. However, I knew that I would be breaking my promise to Jesus, so I held my ground. My poor parents were worried about our country and so was I, but I was not willing to break my promise to Jesus.

"Philomena!" my father shouted at me. "You will marry the Emperor or I will have you work like a servant in our household!"

I did not shudder. Instead, I calmly said, "I will work all the days of my life rather then offend God."

My mother begged me saying, "You will rule the Roman Empire! You would be the most important woman in the world! You will have clothes and jewels beyond compare and servants by the hundreds. You would make us so proud as your mother and father, and you would be protecting your people!"

I did not weaken; rather I said firmly, "God is my Father and Heaven my mother. I wish only to please them, for God and Heaven come before even you, my earthly mother and father."

Of course, I prayed for strength every moment of the day. I spent many hours in the church asking God's pardon for my parents and vigor to withstand their desires for me to marry the Emperor. I begged Heaven for graces and for the Holy Spirit's power to guide me every day of my life.

The next day the attacks were renewed with new effort. I never could have made it through the time of trial without the Holy Spirit's everlasting graces and abundant blessings.

"You will be saving your kingdom by marrying Emperor Diocletian!" my mother said in a loud voice.

I simply replied, "My kingdom is Heaven, mother."

"Think then of our people!" my father shouted. "What will they think of you when we are crushed by the Roman Empire?"

"Whatever they think, they would surely understand that my vow of my virginity to God comes before all else," I said honestly.

Then my mother began to use caresses and comforting words to try to sway me but to no avail. I was sure of my decision and they were weakening quickly. However, they knew what refusal to the Emperor would mean; war, the thing they wished most to avoid. I felt sad for my parents, but I knew that Jesus would rather I disobey my parents then break a sacred vow I made to Him.

The days wore on but my life never returned to its carefree ways. I, who used to spend hours on the beach, remained in my room. Instead of running throughout the palace, I spent hours in the church praying. The times my father and I would ride together were spent threatening me or trying to persuade me in my decision. The fun times I used to spend with my dear mother in the gardens or weaving with the other women in the palace were spent arguing about marrying the Emperor of Rome.

I grew weary every day too, but somehow I continued to stand strong, until finally my parents began to consider the alternative options. I felt truly sorry for them, my parents who had always wanted the best for me. I knew that they thought this was what was best for me, but I also knew that it would be a sin to marry the pagan Emperor.

One night, as I lay in bed, I heard my parents talking in hushed tones. I strained to hear and finally made out voices in the next room.

"She is so stubborn!" my mother said.

"I wonder why?" There was no mistaking the sarcasm in my father's voice. He was known for being a little stubborn and it appeared to have rubbed off on me.

I could picture my dear mother smiling as I heard her pick up her brush and begin on her hair.

"What will we do?" my mother asked after a time of silence. She put her brush down and got into bed.

I heard my father sigh and get into bed as well.

Finally he said, "We will keep begging her and begin preparations for war."

We were only home a few weeks when the next invitation arrived from Rome. The Emperor had heard of my refusals to marry him as well as my wishes to remain a virgin and demanded that I appear before him.

During the preparation days for our journey, I spent many hours in prayer and in solitude asking God's pardon for any sins, and for those of my parents due to my decision. I prayed that the Holy Spirit would continue to guide me and that I would always do my best to please God.

Before we left the island, I bid my friends goodbye and spent an entire hour on the beach collecting shells and simply enjoying the sea air and the water on my toes. Little did I know that the next time I would see my beloved homeland and my people would be from above, beside my Heavenly Spouse.

This time the entourage was smaller and the journey quicker. The whole time my parents were pleading with me to change my mind. It was difficult because we were traveling and I had no place to go and be alone with my thoughts.

When we reached the palace, there was fanfare just as there had been before, as was custom to greet the Emperor's esteemed guests. I was not nervous or worried but my mother did not look quite like herself that day. My parents were both unusually tired looking and weak and I sensed that both had accepted defeat and would now side with the Emperor against me. Still, I did not regret my decision. I knew that the Holy Spirit would help me and put words into my mouth when the time was right.

CHAPTER EIGHT
The Emperor's Fury

When we reached the doors to the palace, we were led to a suite of rooms. Once alone my parents pleaded with me and finally, seeing my resolve, fell on their knees before me.

"No, I cannot marry him!" I replied. "My virginity to God comes before all else!"

As we entered the great throne room once

more, I began to pray more fervently then ever.

Lord Jesus, give me strength! Lord Jesus, give me strength! My heart pounded. I felt anything but strong and courageous, but somehow I knew that my Heavenly Spouse would hear my plea and give me the graces necessary to endure my trial.

As we neared the Emperor, I felt his gaze, and I cringed ever so slightly.

Hear my prayer, dearest Lord! I kept praying as I continued to walk with my eyes fixed on the wall behind the Emperor's throne.

As we bowed before the Emperor, I felt extremely confident that Jesus would hear and answer my prayers as He saw fit.

"Rise!" Emperor Diocletian's deep voice came from above us. "What is this I hear about your refusals to marry me, little princess?"

"I have no wish to marry…" I began but my father cut me off.

"Your Majesty, my daughter refuses to yield to my wishes and I brought her here in hopes that you could change her childish mind," my own father said in a rebuking tone.

"Ah, Princess Philomena dear," the Emperor said to me as we stood before him, "why will you not marry me? I am the richest and most powerful man in the universe!"

God fills that role, I thought. However, I stood with my shoulders back, made eye contact with him and spoke in a loud and clear voice.

"I will not marry you for three reasons: first, because you already have a wife, second, because I do not care for you because of your religious beliefs; and third, because I promised my virginity to Jesus Christ, and I intend to keep that vow until the end of my life on this earth," I declared.

I saw a change in the Emperor's mood as I was speaking. Once I was finished, silence engulfed the whole room.

"And you approved of this...this offering?" Diocletian accused my father, clearly feeling provoked.

"I never approved of her self-sacrifice," my father said defensibly.

"Nor I, Emperor Diocletian," my mother put in, her features reflecting sadness and agony over the entire interrogation.

The Emperor decided to try again, "Well, my little princess, why don't you want to be the Empress of the Roman Empire and save your dear people from destruction?" His tone betrayed his evil plot and I quickly realized just how horrible this man truly was.

"I will not be your Empress or your wife because I am already vowed to another," I replied.

"Your God would be pleased if you were on the throne," the Emperor said, trying to blind me from the true good.

"You lie most definitely," I told him, my voice still remarkably clear and sturdy.

He leaned forward in his throne and looking into my serene face, realized that his charms would not work on me. Therefore, he used threats, promises of curses from his false gods and anything he could think of that would frighten me into marrying him.

None of his threats scared me or made me doubt Jesus and the truth. At times, I felt like weeping from exhaustion but I never ran short on words to object to his evil tactics. I knew it was the work of the Holy Spirit as I bravely defended my virtue, my homeland, and my faith while my parents stood in silence.

When Diocletian finally sat back on his

throne, I thought that perhaps I had won.

Then, words from a man clearly under the influence of the devil came from the silence.

"If you will not have me as a lover, you will have me as a tyrant!" the Emperor shouted, rising to his feet.

There it was; the final threat. I answered firmly with my voice raised only slightly so as not to appear frightened.

"I neither care for you as a lover nor fear you as a tyrant!"

At this, the Emperor's face turned a dark shade of red and he bellowed at the nearby guards, "Throw her into the dungeon below the Imperial Armory, and load her with the heaviest chains!"

My mother gasped, and my father looked faint, but both faces still pleaded with me to change my mind. I could sense their deep sorrow as they watched me, their only child, being sentenced by the Emperor.

I need You so much right now, Lord Jesus! Help my parents! Keep my parents and my people safe! I prayed as I took the chains silently.

I was thrown into a dark, damp cell below the Imperial Armory. The guards sneered that I was a little Grecian princess in a dark Roman cell, and then they left me alone. I prayed for hours until finally I looked up at the tiny window and realized it was night.

CHAPTER NINE
Our Lady's Promise
to Philomena

When Diocletian ordered my chains to be un-
done after several days of pain and suffering, I
was relieved yet wary, because I knew it was

not the end.

Every day for thirty-five days the tyrant came to my cell to renew his offer, and every day I refused. My purity would have been in danger from his attacks had it not been for the protection of my Divine Spouse. I never ceased to offer myself to Jesus and His most loving Mother.

Every day that passed I grew more and more determined to preserve my chastity for the love of my Jesus. Every day that passed I grew more and more reliant on my faith to get me through to the next day.

No one ever told me where my parents were, and I prayed hard for them and my country. Most especially, I prayed for my father, who had never wanted to be apart from me.

I was fed stale bread and water once a day. The guards were cruel and did not care if my one 'meal' was late. They never offered me an extra blanket so instead I learned to live with my one threadbare rag that I had found in the cell.

Days continued to pass, and I wondered if I was ever again to walk beneath the blue sky or hear my parents' or my friends' voices. All I could see from my window was a small patch of sky, and all I could hear were the gruff voices of Romans on the street.

On the thirty-seventh day of my imprisonment, a strange light began to form in my dark cell. I saw the Blessed Virgin Mary appear out of the light holding in her arms the Infant Jesus. I fell on my knees before this glorious vision. Our Lady was dressed in radiant garments befitting a queen, and her Divine Son smiled with a childlike joy. From both radiated a light so unearthly and bright that I later wondered why my guard had not been alerted.

"My daughter," she said to me, "three days more of prison and after forty days you shall leave this state of pain."

At her words, my heart suddenly filled with happiness. I was to see my parents and my homeland again!

Then Our Lady went on to describe the dreadful torments I would still have to endure. I fell into the most horrible agony that I was sure would be my death as I heard her words. The small hope I had formed of being free vanished into the darkness.

"Have courage, my child," Mary then said to me. "Are you unaware of the love of predilection that I bear for you? The name, which you received in baptism, is the pledge of it for the resemblance which it has to that of my Son and to mine. You are called Lumena, as Your Spouse is called Light, Star, Sun, as I myself am called Aurora, Star, the Moon in the fullness of its brightness, and Sun. Fear not, I will aid you. Now nature, whose weakness humbles you, asserts its law. In the moment of combat, grace will come to lend you its force, and your Angel, who was also mine, Gabriel, whose name expresses strength, will come to your aid. I will recommend you especially to his care, as the well beloved among my children."[1]

These words from the Queen of Heaven restored my vigor and courage. The vision disappeared, leaving behind a heavenly fragrance in my previously dismal cell.

What my Blessed Mother had prepared me for was soon to take place, and I began to arm myself with unceasing prayers and praise of God.

---

1   Quoted in Miravalle, *It's Time to Meet St. Philomena.*

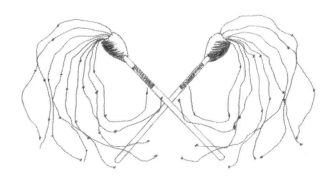

CHAPTER TEN
Torture at the Hands of the Emperor

Diocletian was determined to break my will and demanded that I be publicly stripped and scourged, just as Our Lady had foretold.

His horrifying words were, "Since you choose to reject my offer of marriage for your so-called King of the Jews, you will be treated as he was treated."

The prison guards were reluctant to unclothe me entirely as they tied me to a great column in the presence of the noblemen in Diocletian's court. I was lashed with cruelty until I was covered in blood; my entire body ached with severe pain. Yet, miraculously, I did not lose consciousness. The whole time I prayed that I would be strong and withstand the cruel scourging that ripped my flesh and caused me to lose my life's blood. The noblemen were as merciless as Diocletian himself. They jeered and laughed at me with hatred while I was scourged. I had never known such brutality as a well-loved princess.

Physically I was in horrible condition. I was stained red from the blood that poured forth from all of my wounds, yet my soul was still as white as the light that had shone from Our Lady three days ago in my cell.

Diocletian had me dragged back to my cell

where he expected me to perish. I prayed that I would die so that I could join my Spouse in Heaven that day but my will was second to God's and I hung onto life. I felt dizzy from the lack of blood and my cell spun around me. I breathed heavily and tried to stay awake long enough to pray for the guards, the noblemen, and Diocletian's salvation. I clung onto consciousness, determined not to sleep until my prayers of forgiveness had ended.

Then two shining angels appeared, and once more, my dim cell was lit by Heaven's purest light. The two angels were dressed in simple white garments and had stunning golden wings. They applied a healing balm onto my wounds, giving me strength that I did not have even before the scourging.

I looked up to thank my heavenly healers, but they were already gone. They had gone back to Heaven, the place I so longed to be with my Spouse.

I am healed! Thank You God! I thought happily, looking at the places that had, just a few moments before, been so bloody and wounded. I felt so grateful and my heart filled with joy. My mood changed instantly as I recalled Our Lady's words that it was not the end. I knew I had so much more to suffer, but a new conviction burned inside me. I was once again willing to face God's plan for me with faith in His perfect love and mercy.

Then I suffered from horrible thoughts in the short time that followed my first torture. *Would the Emperor continue to try to persuade me to marry him? Where were my parents? Did they know about the cruel scourging that I had endured by God's grace? Did they leave and return to Corfu without me? Had my own parents who loved me so much abandoned me?*

Then I had some more thoughts, but they

were not doubts. *God is with me. Jesus is also with me, so I have nothing to fear. I must not forget Our Lady's promise that she would send Archangel Gabriel to my aid.*

Diocletian heard of my healing and had me brought before him, determined to prove that it was his false god, Jupiter, who had cured me. He told me that it meant that I was destined to become the Empress of the Roman Empire.

In turn, I stood before him shaking my head and telling him repeatedly, "I worship only Jesus Christ, my healer and His Father, my Creator."

His fury grew more and more intense and yet I remained calm and serene.

"I will break your resolution if it is the last thing I do, little princess!" he sneered at me.

I tilted my chin to meet him eye to eye and said, "You may try to break me, but it will be because of God's grace that I will stand strong against you."

CHAPTER ELEVEN
At the Bottom of the Tiber River

The Emperor was furious, because once again I had bested him with Heaven's unfailing help. He could do nothing but torture me until I begged for mercy, renounced my faith, and agreed to marry him or simply died. My determination to remain strong would not save me from the Emperor's tortures.

A few days later, I was brought from my cell, my hands bound tightly behind me, to the center of a bridge that spanned over the Tiber River. There was a large crowd already gathered there, and I knew they were waiting to see the Grecian princess drowned for her Christian faith. I silently prayed for their souls. I also prayed for my own soul and any wrongdoings that I may have committed and asked God's pardon.

The guards dragged a heavy anchor forward and fastened it with a rope around my neck. Then they set me on the ledge of the bridge. I looked down into the water of the river below and then up to Heaven. I felt confident that the Archangel Gabriel would help me as I faced drowning.

Diocletian gave the order to cast me into the

river. The guards obeyed, heaving the heavy anchor onto the ledge. *God,* I prayed, *help me!* As I finished my brief prayer, the two guards pushed the anchor over the side of the bridge. I quickly plunged into the cool water below but I did not reach the muddy river bottom as I had expected. Instead, I saw an immaculate and heavenly light begin to form in the dark waters of the Tiber.

God, in all His mercy, sent two angels once again to save me from the tyrant's wrath. They untied the anchor and, in plain sight, brought me back to the surface. The crowd stared in awe as I was placed gently on the riverbank.

I was not harmed or even slightly wet.

The Emperor was horribly infuriated as the multitude of people loudly rejoiced. Many people converted to Christianity that day as they looked upon me, a princess saved by God from certain death.

Diocletian was convinced I possessed magical powers that were saving me from his tortures, both physically and spiritually. By God's grace I had persevered, and Diocletian looked ridiculous. His own subjects were converting despite his obsession to break my vow of purity.

Once again, I missed watching the angels ascend back into Heaven, the place I so longed to be for all eternity. Still, I simply stood and smiled as the people proclaimed their faith in the one true God.

I was well aware of what would follow: more torture, more prison, and eventually death. However, I reminded myself that I was under Our Lady's mantle and would remain there forever, wrapped in her heavenly love.

I was not even returned to my cell. The guards held me while the crowd was rounded up and taken to the dungeons.

Poor people, I thought, *accused of being Christian even before they are baptized, and just because they believe in a miracle!*

This did not slow down my cruel persecutor. As he was about to order another group to be thrown in the dungeons, I received heavenly inspiration.

I gathered my thoughts and shouted them at the tyrant who was about five yards away from me. "You fool! They are not baptized, so they are not yet true Christians! Throwing innocent people into your dungeons out of spite for me is a cowardly thing to do."

Diocletian turned to me with wickedness showing clearly on his face.

"And how do you know that they are innocent of Christianity?" he asked, rage resounding in his voice.

"It is impossible to be guilty of something

that you know nothing about," I replied, fueled by the Holy Spirit. My temper flared at the injustices of Diocletian. My heart raced silently inside me as I publicly challenged the tyrant.

"One hour with you and all these people would surely be Christians," he replied, annoyed with my outbursts but even more furious because I was right.

"Only a heartless and cruel man would condemn innocent people to death for simply seeing something that is of God!" I shouted at him. The guards' hold on my arms loosened as they listened with amazement at my nerve.

I stood straight and tall as the Emperor spoke, "Silence her with arrows as she is dragged through the streets of Rome!"

I lifted my chin as I was led away to meet my fate.

CHAPTER TWELVE
Pierced by the Arrows

I knew that the next torture would be far worse than the Tiber River. The thought of being tied behind a horse-drawn wagon and dragged through the streets of Rome while being shot at with arrows scared me. Still, I gave myself to Jesus as the guards held me, waiting for the wagon to pull up.

The wagon arrived several moments later, and a tremor of fear made me shake. The horse was skittish and large, but I reminded myself that I was Jesus' spouse. The guards bound my hands to the wagon tightly, and the ropes cut into my flesh. The dirt and brick roads scraped me as I was dragged forward. Archers lined up and began to fire arrows at me. The arrows fell on me like a rain shower, piercing my skin. My blood flowed abundantly, but I did not faint. I prayed to Jesus, reminding myself of His agony on the way to Calvary.

The arrows finally ceased and the same guards carried me back to my cell where Diocletian, once again, expected me to die. My wounds were severe but I recalled Our Lady's words that there was more to suffer. Before I could remember the next torture that was to come, I fell into a heavenly sleep that restored my health and cured me of my injuries. When I awoke, my vigor was renewed and I wasted no time in thanking Jesus for my healings.

It was not long before Diocletian found out about my healing. He assembled the archers and, once more, I was bound. I was made to stand with my back against a wall, facing the archers straight on.

I knew that Archangel Gabriel was there with me as I awaited the sharp arrows. I prayed for my torturers and my own soul as the archers bent their bows, all the arrows aimed at me.

One word from the Emperor and all the strings were released. I inhaled sharply, bracing myself against the impending pain, but felt nothing. The arrows had not left the bows at all! I had to smile at my dear Spouse's sense of humor as Diocletian's face became red.

"Make the tips of the arrows red-hot, for fire

is the only way to overcome such magic!" Diocletian ordered.

While the archers scrambled to obey his orders, I took notice of the vast crowd. They were quiet compared to the other crowds that had gathered to see me tortured. I felt sure that they were waiting for more miracles. I loved them for their faith in the one true God, whom they did not really know. I knew, as well as they did, that it was likely they would be thrown into prison.

Finally, the arrows were ready, and the archers lined up again. All of the arrows were aimed at my heart. I was not afraid, for I knew Heaven would save me if it was God's will.

For the third time, the archers let go of the arrows. The hot tips flew toward my heart but stopped halfway and turned to strike those who had fired them. Those gathered gasped as I prayed for the souls of the six archers who had just died. The archers who were left looked pale as a vast number of people renounced their pagan beliefs, and Diocletian looked on in disgust.

I lifted my eyes toward Heaven and offered a silent prayer of thanksgiving.

CHAPTER THIRTEEN
On Her Way to Heaven

As the crowd and archers proclaimed their belief in God, Emperor Diocletian hurled various curses at me. I stood silently, still bound and still grinning. While the Emperor yelled at me, the crowd managed to get away peacefully.

Diocletian was furious with me but I remained unfazed.

"Take her back into the palace and behead her!" the tyrant ordered. "Let us see if her God can save her from death now!"

I knew that God wanted me with Him and that I was going to die. I went with the guards smiling, for I knew I would be in Heaven within the hour.

The guards brought me inside a small, dark room with stone walls. There was a block of wood in the middle of the room, and they set me before it. Diocletian stood to the side as I knelt, awaiting my death.

"This is your last chance, little princess!" he sneered at me.

"I choose Jesus," I replied without any hesitation. "I forgive you, Emperor Diocletian."

Diocletian, enraged by my final words of forgiveness, killed me, ending my short life on earth.

My soul ascended into Heaven on a Friday in 304 A.D. in the third hour after midday. I had suffered, survived and died, all for my Heavenly Spouse, who welcomed me Himself at the marvelous gates into eternal life.

I was given the crown of virginity and a palm to symbolize my martyrdom.

How joyous I was the day I entered into Heaven, greeted by other martyrs who had also been killed under Diocletian! How happy I was to come face to face with Jesus Christ after my long period of affliction on earth! How much I loved my special blessing from my Spouse: the title Saint Philomena, Powerful with God!

That is my story. I will always be with those who need help preserving their purity. Ask me, and in turn, I shall ask my Heavenly Father, for I am refused nothing. Be aware: purity is one of God's most magnificent gifts to us, and it is so important to treasure and guard it as though it is a precious gem.

Saint Philomena,
Powerful with God

PART TWO
Worldwide Devotions to Saint Philomena

THE CORD

The Cord of St. Philomena is approved by the Congregation of Rites. It is used by many people who are devoted to St. Philomena to guard purity, as a protection from temptations, and accidents as well as to obtain cures from sicknesses. The red and white Cord is made out of either wool, linen or cotton thread. The red symbolizes martyrdom and the white symbolizes virginity. It is worn under a person's clothing and should be blessed beforehand. Those who wear the Cord are to say the following prayer every day:

> *O St. Philomena, virgin and martyr, pray for us that, through thy powerful intercession, we may obtain that purity of mind and heart which leads to the perfect love of God. Amen.*

Pope Leo XIII, in 1893, granted 100 days' indulgence to the faithful who wear the Cord of St. Philomena and recite the above prayer with devotion everyday. Plenary indulgences are granted on five certain occasions to those who faithfully wear the Cord. Those days are:

1. On the day on which the Cord is worn the first time

2. On May 25, the anniversary of the discovery of the body of St. Philomena in the Catacomb of St. Priscilla

3. On August 11, feast of St. Philomena

4. On December 15, the anniversary of the approbation of the Cord by the Holy See

5. At the moment of death, under the ordinary conditions

Prayer to be said while putting on the Cord for the first time:

O St. Philomena, who hast endured death for the sake of Jesus Christ, graciously obtain for me patience in this illness, and if it is the will of God, grant that on putting on this Cord, blest in thy honor, I may recover health of body, in order to labor with greater fervor for the sanctification of my soul. Amen.

Saint Philomena

BLESSED OIL

In 1805, the mother of a blind child was at the shrine of St. Philomena in Mugnano, Italy. She dipped her fingers into a lamp, one of the many that burn perpetually before the remains of the saint. The mother applied the oil to her blind child's eyelids and the child was immediately able to see. Since that time numerous reports of physical healings have occurred, and the devotion to the oil of St. Philomena has become widely known. People have been healed of illnesses, night terrors, deafness, blindness and many other afflictions.

The blessed oil can be obtained on line: **www.shopphilomena.com**

The oil comes directly from the Shrine of St. Philomena in Mugnano, Italy. All sales of items from this site go directly to support the upkeep of the Sanctuary of St. Philomena in Mugnano.

THE NOVENA

To be said on nine consecutive days.

O great Saint Philomena, glorious Virgin and
Martyr, obtain for me purity of body and soul,
purity of heart and desire, purity of thought
and affection. Through the patient endurance
you showed under the weight of great sufferings, obtain for me a submissive acceptance of
all the afflictions God may lovingly allow me

to endure. May I pass through the waters of trial and distress without detriment to my soul and may I glorify the Lord as He helps me to grow in virtue and grace. In addition to these requests, obtain for me, O faithful spouse of Jesus, the particular intention I wholeheartedly entrust to you at this moment. O pure Virgin and holy Martyr, turn your Heavenly face towards me your devoted servant; comfort me in affliction, assist me in danger, and above all come to my aid in the hour of death. Watch over the interests of the Church of God, prayer for its exaltation and prosperity, the spreading of the Catholic faith, for the Pope, for the clergy, for the perseverance of the faithful, the conversion of sinners, the return of fallen away Catholics, and the relief of the souls in purgatory. O great Saint Philomena intercede for me, that I may one day look upon the glorious crown bestowed on you in

Heaven, and eternally bless the Lord who so abundantly rewards for all eternity the sufferings endured for love of Him during this short life. Amen.

Saint Philomena

A SHORT
PRAYER
to St. Philomena

by Courtney, Age Eight

Dear Saint Philomena, please keep us safe from bad thoughts, bad dreams, bad people and anything else that might come between us and God, us and each other, us and life and us and love. Amen.

Saint Philomena

I say this prayer right before falling asleep every night. "Us" refers to my family but you could just pray it for yourself.

SHRINE
of Saint Philomena
Mugnano, Italy

St. Philomena's shrine is located twenty miles northeast of Naples in Mugnano, Italy. The Shrine is also referred to as 'Saint Philomena's Sanctuary.' The remains of St. Philomena were brought to Mugnano from Rome in 1805, about three years after their discovery. Many miracles have taken place at the shrine and continue to occur.

Santuario Santa Filomena

Rettor Sac Giovanni Filomena

83027 Mugnano Del Cardinale,

Avellino, Italy

FEAST DAY
of St. Philomena
August 11th

There have been some misunderstandings regarding St. Philomena's Feast Day. This confusion arose from a decision made by the Sacred Congregation of Rites in 1961. This liturgical directive removed many traditional feasts honoring Jesus, Mary and various saints from the liturgical calendar. St. Philomena was among those removed. This action was in no way a denial of her sainthood. It did not in any way discourage or suspend public or private devotion to St. Philomena.

ABOUT THE AUTHOR

My connection to St. Philomena began before I was born. My mom had a rough pregnancy with me, and my grandma (we affectionately call her Nan) prayed to St. Philomena that my mom and I would be all right. The doctors had repeatedly told my mom that my kidneys were too small and that I might be born with

Down syndrome. No one told my mom that I could die during birth, but the doctor told my Nan, who was in the waiting room. She stormed Heaven for a miracle. On February 22, 1998 around six in the morning, I was born. I was only six pounds, one ounce and not even sixteen inches long, and I was completely healthy.

When it came time to pick a confirmation saint when I was nine, I did not hesitate; I chose St. Philomena.

For years after my confirmation, my family urged me to write a book about St. Philomena. I finally decided to do it when I was thirteen. I knew if I was going to write a book about Philomena, I wanted to write it while I was thirteen, the age Philomena was when she was martyred. I began in September of 2011 and the first draft was finished by December. It was a long, hard process, but one that was full of blessings for me and my family.

I don't know everything about St. Philomena, but I know that she is a great saint. She has been an inspiration and a role model to me and many others for over two centuries now, and will continue to be until the end of time.

Courtney Catherine Filomena Lee

Saint Philomena

Bibliography

Carroll, Anne. *Christ the King Lord of History.* Illinois: Tan Books and Publishers Inc., 1994.

Miravalle, Mark. *It is time to meet St. Philomena.* California: Queenship Publishing Company, 2007.

Mohr, Sister Marie Helene. *Saint Philomena Powerful with God.* Illinois: Tan Books and Publishers Inc, 1988.

Saint Philomena

O'Sullivan, Fr. Paul. *Saint Philomena the Wonder-Worker*. Illinois: Tan Books and Publishers Inc., 1993.

More Information

For more information, please visit us at

www.saintphilomena.net

Resellers:

Wholesale orders for this book can be placed at

www.createspace.com/pub/l/createspacedirect.do

89419723R00071

Made in the USA
San Bernardino, CA
25 September 2018